Little Altars

Little Altars

Poems by

Bonnie Wehle

Cover image by Roxana Zemi
Author photo by Ana Blum

ISBN: 978-1-63980-676-8

Kelsay Books
502 South 1040 East, A-119
American Fork, Utah 84003
Kelsaybooks.com

Memory is a complicated thing,
a relative to truth, but not its twin.
—*Barbara Kingsolver*

Acknowledgments

The author is grateful to the following journals and anthologies for publishing the following poems, sometimes in a slightly different version:

The Avocet: "Early Morning Ride"
Black Coffee Review: "Do Not Resuscitate"
Coal Hill Review: "Self-Portrait as a Trout," "Postcard from New York"
Her Words/Black Mountain Press: "Nomenclature"
The Ocotillo Review: "On Edge," "Beachcombing"
orangepeel: "Painting My Portrait in the Style of Frida"
River Heron Review: "Perhaps a Peach"
Rockvale Review: "Conjunction: 1997"
Sandcutters: "Day of the Dead," "Longevity," "Waiting for Words"
When a Woman Tells the Truth: Writings and Creative Work by Women Over 80: "Bar Codes"

My deepest gratitude goes to my many teachers for their wisdom, guidance and encouragement, and to my fellow poets who have been so generous with their insightful comments and suggestions.

Contents

Day of the Dead

We watch families arrange treasures on little altars
to entice their lost beloveds to return for a visit

and you ask what I want on mine. I remind you
that each poem I write is a shrine on which I gather

what survives, where I probe my mind for truth, dig
for forgotten fragments buried deep in my brain,

like chipping ore from the wall of an old mine,
the pickaxe sharpened, wielded with caution,

unearthing celadon, nuggets of turquoise, jade,
a rusty shovel, a miner's lamp missing its wick.

Put these on my altar.

Learning the Lyrics

I float in her body,
its shape a swelling
she would not tolerate
under other circumstances.

Curled in on myself,
I hear a refrain belted
by the ardent lungs above me,
With someone like you,
a pal so good and true . . .

lyrics I will learn in a Buick
convertible with the top down,
on driving trips to nowhere.
We'll find a perfect peace,
where joys will never cease . . .

before her brown curls dull,
brown eyes dim,
before we discover those lungs
will be her undoing,

scar over, fail,
the life she gave breath
holding tight to songs
missing verses.

Nomenclature

after Roger Bonair-Agard

In the language of childhood,
my name meant dark purple lilacs,
horses, the fragrance of a barn.
It meant the caress of grass on bare feet.

My mother's name meant sorrow,
never whole, hard to breathe.
My mother gave me my name.
She meant to give me hers.

My name means lovely in Scottish,
in French, good.
I no longer know my name.
I no longer speak those languages.

My mother taught me to talk
with words for fear, worry, tears.
She sang me lullabies
in the language of her fractured lungs.

In my language, my name means woman
who whistles in the dark.
It means truth buried in metaphor,
light tinged with shadow.

Camera Angle

She gazes directly at the Kodak Brownie
gripped by an unknown photographer
who views its upside-down image from above.

No matter how long I stare at the photo—
its torn edges, yellow patches on the back
where tape held it on the album page—
I cannot bring life to her face

though I know it as I know my own—
its level brow, high cheekbones, narrow lips,
which sometimes smile, but rarely laugh.
It's the eyes that bother,
that refuse to shed tears,
reveal sorrows, or dreams
of folding into a mother's arms.

I see her through a lens that exposes
the ghost of a scowl, the clenched jaw,
the tightly held mouth that says,
I'm fine, I'm perfectly fine,
as her lips curl into a counterfeit smile.

And I know the little girl who stands beside her,
ebbs into her shadow,
to lean against a shoulder that isn't there.

On Edge

It's not heights that frighten me,
it's edges,
where the falls start—
too close to the canyon rim,
where my mother,
always perched on the edge
of emotional collapse,
grabbed the back of my shirt,
held on as if grappling
with sanity itself.
I did the same to my children,
to my sanity.
Maybe it's genetic, this struggle.

Crouched atop a narrow
scaffold two stories up, I study
round cheeks—
a ceiling of painted cherubs,
wings of gold that need re-gilding.
On hands and knees,
I squeeze the railing, viselike,
anxiety pricking at my palms.
The descent holds terror.
Don't look down, I tell myself.

I stare into the faces of the putti,
their puerile smiles more
like grimaces,
like challenges—
disguised disdain for the unnerved.
They have been here for decades,
winged, yet fixed firmly in place,
and I, earth-weighted,
as stuck as they are.

Perhaps a Peach

What I recalled was carving words
into the top of the antique pine table
with a groundhog's tooth,
an odd object for defacing the surface
on which we ate each meal.

Why did this come to mind while reading Li-Young Lee?
His poem about eating peaches,
taking what we love inside us,
so different from violating an heirloom
with the incisor of a deceased beast
at that table meant as an altar of family communion,
eating perhaps a peach, which for Lee,
held within its skin days of ripening in the sun, joy.
For us, mouthfuls of moist peach flesh
conveniently quashing speech.

What do I remember of that ill-treated table
other than my abuse of it,
other than mutely eaten meals,
our family its veneer,
me breaking the hush with a rodent's cuspid?
O, silence in need of sound.

Changing Trains

because when our parents separate, Mother's doctor
advises her to move to Arizona

because a black porter in a white jacket
transforms sofas into beds with crisp white sheets

because in Chicago we transfer from the New York Central
to the Southern Pacific

because the scenery transmutes from backyard clotheslines
and weedy lots to a horizon of wheat, corn, soybeans

because at night passing trains strobe light and dark
into our windows to the clackity cadence of their wheels

because it's sand and sagebrush now, distant hills,
mountains, bluish, muted

because we are transfixed by Native women in tribal dress,
clay pots displayed in the laps of patient grandmothers

because in Tucson Mother sings, laughs,
but still coughs.

The Dreamers

When you were five, you kept garter snakes in your pinafore pocket. Nothing sinister, just for the companionship, took them out now and then, let them slither across your flattened palms, quickly replacing the edge of one hand with the edge of the other. The reptiles, like childhood dreams, got nowhere, ended up back in your pocket. That wasn't all. There were tiny painted turtles, and several lizards, kept in various vessels on the sill. They baked in the sun, I imagine, and when the rain beat on the window leaving wet trails on the panes, greenish from the reflected lawn, they must have dreamt of rivers with lush banks. Fresh air. Freedom. They all eventually disappeared into the geological folds of your bedroom, excavated years later, no doubt, by insect archaeologists, who, finding their ancient bones, gave them Latin names, mostly ending in *saurus*. Your sister dreamt of palaces and princes, spent her days immersed in tales of armored knights, velvet robes, diamond tiaras, the stack of books on the floor by her bed, the tower, perhaps, from which she let down her braids. Nowadays she lives on acreage in Northern California, filled with chickens, goats, geese, a garden she tends by herself. She loves the feel of the soil in her hands, writes notes on the squash leaves, so the pendulous fruit grows to mythic proportions. But there are nights when her geese become steaming white steeds, the feed bucket, a golden carriage. There are plenty of mice for coachmen. Your parents, of course, had high hopes—father and mother each with separate dreams. Though you had no idea what they might have been—trust me, they were largely unfulfilled.

Early Morning Ride

water droplets hang in hazy air
hush disturbed by a crush
of horses' hooves on last year's leaves
field glasses slung as weaponry
     we listen and watch
shadow broken by sunglow
     stillness in light
     stirring in dark
sudden flights of color
     Scarlet Tanager
     Indigo Bunting
     Golden-winged Warbler
these are what we've come for
     father and I
     rare birds

Mean Girl

The day was cloudless,
no storms expected.
Her sisters, mine, sprawled
on blanket-spread turf,
cookies, lemonade.
In the house, her parents, mine,
alcohol, glasses, glances.

I don't recall her name
or how old she was, four, maybe five,
a bit younger than me, the girl
I kept slapping, slapping, slapping,
her curly hair, brown eyes
and brows so like my own,
her cheeks getting redder, redder.

Then the parents,
running to discover who the screamer,
who the sinner.
I, the naughty child, scolded
by my handsome father, the lady's man,
the begetter of girls.

Did I know, even then, who the sinner?

Self-Portrait as a Trout

How often I have played the part of this poor fish
skewered by a barbed hook it mistook
for something benign,
lying here on this bloody board
mouth and gills opening and closing,
tail still trying to rudder it to safety.
It's no use.

My father wants to show me how to clean my catch.
His long fingers, with their carefully tended nails,
insert a sharp, pointed knife, deftly
into the belly of the fish just behind the gills.
An unrepentant assassin, he draws the blade
swiftly back toward the tail.
Pale pink coils tumble onto the board.

He eases the flesh from the bone,
then from the skin, produces two
perfect filets he will dip into milk,
dredge in flour,
then fry in his favorite pan
hanging above us from an iron hook.
Still, I watch for barbs.

Late September

A familiar route I have not taken for years,
leads me past meadows of mown timothy
bordered by dense hedgerows.
Small orbs crowd the crowns of the apple trees.
Their fallen fellows clutter the earth below,
fill the air with the vinegary scent of rotting fruit.

This was my father's place.
The log cabin, stone house, and barns
he built all remain. The split-rail fences
still stand, though they need repair.
Fences, like family ties, can be fragile.

I follow the haphazard edges for nearly a mile.
As I walk, my eyes tear unexpectedly,
black and white memories take on color.
I pass beneath a sugar maple, its leaves
wave to the ground around me,
orange, yellow, red.

Water Sign

Don't go near the water.
Quicksand, you say,
a deception for my own good.
At four, I believe
everything you tell me, Father,
no matter how many times you lie.

Years later I tumble into the deep end,
a tan body arrows after me,
soft towels wrap my shaking shoulders,
there's the comforting chatter of women.
I was born under the sign of the crab—
water should be my element.

In mid-twenties, as the sailboat rights,
the bilge board catches my life belt,
drags me down, down.
I push free, thrash upward,
break the surface, gasping.
Later, the squall returns.

At fifty, my mask leaks, snorkel catches water.
He who vowed eternal love tells me
he loves another.
We were warned not to step on the coral.
I need solid footing,
something I can trust.

The Pretender

When he said, *So, tell me about yourself,*
I turned to make sure my shadow
was still attached, flat, colorless, vaguely
body shaped. Like a paper doll.

My skin seems to stretch more tidily
around the bones of others than it does my own.
My thoughts cradle better in someone else's brain,
spring more easily from someone else's mouth.
I prefer to write in someone else's voice.

You may hear me from the next room
reciting lines assigned to the dead or distant,
searching for myself on random gravestones,
in portraits painted with raucous colors
I recognize from somewhere.

Through a crack in my wall,
you can watch me cut dolls from cardboard,
shut them in a drawer
and double lock the door behind me.

Painting My Portrait in the Style of Frida

I choose a thin board
that has already seen some use. Apply
gray primer liberally, then coat

each inch of the surface
in a thick impasto of bold colors.
I don't hold back.

I paint the mirror image
turned a bit to one side
so the face is partly in shadow.

With the tip of my brush, I tease
the downturned lips into a faint smile,
paint over any revealed emotions.

I add flowers, birds, small animals
as distractions—lots of them—
around the face, earrings, necklaces,

scarves, and ribbons, both pink and red.
Yes, that should nicely mask
the doubt and longing.

I soften the hard edges with my finger,
then resist the temptation to lay in the past
as background. Instead

I dab in some cacti—prickly pear—
and with a pointed brush
carefully stroke on thorns—lots of them.

Genetic Predisposition

My mother was good at keeping secrets
—especially hers.
You don't have to tell everything you know,
she'd warn. And she didn't.
Friends learned not to press her
but hoped for an opening—
a breath of intimacy from her tubercular lungs.

New friends and I gather for wine,
conversation.
We don't know each other's lives,
those years before we met—
hobbies, passions, travels—
before our world shrank
to yesterday and tomorrow.
Our news is the immediate—
recent surgeries, last night's dinner.

But they too want more,
probe each other for indiscretions,
lovers, affairs.
They want secrets and are willing to share.
So, what about you? They ask.
But they will learn
I am my mother's daughter.

Family Recipe

In a blue plastic binder on my cookbook shelf
is a typewritten recipe for salmon mousse
given to my mother by a man who catered her parties.
Absent from the page, is the story of when he prepared it
in the nude, forgot to put the lid on the blender
and the pink mixture erupted all over his body.
Also missing, are years of repeating the tale,
the rare, shared laughter it always brought.
Other stories are not amusing. On the pages
of my memory are a mother's sobs as, once again,
she chooses sadness over joy. These are the narratives
I return to as if their retelling could set them right.
But the binder has no recipe for how to unsee her tears,
no recipe for unfeeling her fears.

Camouflage

There are perils in revealing ourselves to others.
The hornworm chomping on the leaves
of my tomato plant matches them
so perfectly that the holes she chews
are the only evidence of her presence.

She doesn't realize she is color-matching,
nor is she aware of the ruin her action spawns.
She troubles only to hump along unnoticed,
make it to the next stage of life
without getting crushed under a gardener's boot,
live to become a hummingbird moth,
flaunt her brown and orange wings.

My sister once accused me of acting differently
with different people. I do, I thought everyone did.
The chameleons I kept in containers as a child
never knew which color would protect them.
They promptly perished.

Slow Burn

I was the first-born, the debutante in the ball gown.
For me the piano lessons, dancing lessons,
new clothes, my own room, painted pink.
She, in the middle, the over-shadowed shadow
I had to look behind me to see,
given my old clothes, no dancing, no piano,
dreamt of glass-slippers that never arrived,
shared her birthday with Christmas,
her bedroom with the youngest,
the baby, the attention-getter.

Sixty years would pass before
the hand-me-down princess,
the never-complaining dreamer,
allowed her bottled resentment to boil over.
Stored anger rolled out of her
like steam from a kettle,
spread across the space between us
until it was the only thing in the room,
the burner beneath the pot, red hot.

Postcard from New York

How like me to think you'd keep that postcard—
that remembrance of a place we'd been together,
though, of course, the towers are missing

and I there missing you
on a bench at a bus stop
on my way to The Met.

Perhaps I should have waited, sent a photo
of *Seated Nude Holding a Flower,*
that Miró painting you always loved
when you loved me, then loved me not—

her ample flesh so yellow, pink, and green
and blue,
that tiny daisy resting on her knee,
its petals still intact.

Beachcombing

I have returned to that beach, where
      in other days you and I strolled back and forth
like the ebb and flow of surf on sand
      not knowing how much to cherish—

strode past calcified shells forsaken
      by the creatures they once sheltered
past dried algae and desiccated fish
      oblivious to the portent of their rotting smell

searched for small, oddly shaped glass shards
      we thought to treasure
their edges worn, their colors muted—
      each piece an elegy.

I tell you this because that shoreline has shifted.
      I no longer know how to move along it
how to comb for delight, to live with desire.
      Yet I walk there now as if I could still step

in the same sandy impressions our feet made
      in those days we embraced
as if there were still two sets of tracks
      moving in the same direction

like other unbroken things—
      the limpet snug in its shell
the shore before the storm
      your soft and steady humming.

Bar Codes

Neil Armstrong had just landed on the moon,
the country was filled with space-shot fervor.
I wore tinfoil antennae
to a dress as-in-the-future costume party
and drew bar codes on my wrists.

What information might those lines reveal
when read by the right device,
my age and weight,
propensity for failing at science,
and love,
likelihood of career success—
a virtual fortune teller who reveals too much.

When a friend entered hospice last week
her doctors gave her only a few days—
but how many exactly?

What information do we want,
what would we rather not know?

Halley's comet crossed within view in 1989.
Astronomers predict it will show up again in 2061.

This morning, I noticed yesterday's hibiscus blossom
had already folded her petals around herself.

To Die with Boots On

He'd saddle Duke, his gray gelding,
and they'd set off together,
he in his Irish fisherman's hat,
a whistle around his neck.

They'd amble with the pointers through oat grass,
timothy, and thistle, ragweed, and brome,
the dogs running ahead, checking back, father's
knee-high boots soaking up the lingering dew.

This was his religion, this communion of man
and horse and dog and wet boots.
The afterlife better include those things,
he'd say, tugging his footwear off at the door.

When a friend's horse returned one day
without its rider, the friend's son found
his father lying on the trail, his hands at his heart,
his dog standing guard.

My father decided that was the way to go
and promised to create it for himself
if a drawn-out death were forecast.
He mapped his plan: hat, boots, loaded gun.

Instead, he lies in a room, gray-walled, stifling,
no horse, no dog, no hat, or boots, saddled
with breathing apparatus, plugs, tubes,
a monitor tracking his heart.

Waiting for Words

My father lies in a bed down the hall.
I sit with strangers in an airless room,
work crossword puzzles in a book I brought along.
W a i t i n g r o o m. In the puzzle it looks like
one word. 2 across, place of anticipation.
No, 4 down, enclosure of apprehension.

The air in the room smells like the onions
someone put on their burger
from the hospital cafeteria.
But stress has a stronger odor.
8 down, six-letter word for rotting vegetable.
I pencil in *s t e n c h.* And keep waiting.

A family whose wait has ended
brings in a vase of flowers,
sets it on the only table and quickly leaves,
hoping, perhaps, to cleanse
a n x i e t y from the room.
11 across, seven-letter word for dread.

Doctors and nurses come to report
to the waiting strangers, talk in hushed tones.
A hall speaker screeches out what no one wants
to hear, eight letters, two words,
one of the things this puzzle
doesn't warn me about. *C o d e b l u e.*

And still I *w a i t.*
17 across, four-letter word for endure.
Or maybe it's *b i d e*—
what one does before one's world changes forever.
5 across, four-letter word for foreboding.
Then, 9 down, five letters, permanent loss of breath.

Do Not Resuscitate

Specific instructions
legalese on a preprinted form
      stowed in a dresser drawer.

On the small pad the nurse placed by your bed
your hand   unsteady   spells out
      What happened to me?

The EMTs didn't wait for the form
they had their instructions.
      No discussion.

You were so adamant, Mother
please   no tubes   no machines.
      The words stuffed down your throat.

I stroke your hand   skin thin as tissue
carry on our one-sided conversation
      dog is fine   grandkids miss you

and struggle with words that stick in my throat
like tomorrow
      next week.

Conjunction: 1997

Day after day, we sorted,
we wrapped, we packed
the accumulation of our mother's life.

Each night I floated alone in her pool.
It was the year the comet Hale-Bopp
appeared in the heavens
brighter than the stars
and the year our mother, who shone
with her own light, disappeared
       from earth.

The comet was visible
with the naked eye, but
       I confronted
the darkness through binoculars
discovered in a desk drawer.
My sister and I had flown
in turns, from our distant homes,
to carry out the arduous work of
       mourning.

Night after night
I watched, exhausted, enthralled,
as the comet, shedding
its enormous trail of dust and debris
       through the cosmos,
made its slow voyage forward
with the same heft
and singleness of purpose
demanded of me,
as I journeyed through
my firmament
       of loss.

Reflections

A quarter-century
in my closet
its quilted, light-blue
satin well-worn.
Chilly mornings
I pull it tight
sit and read
in front of my fake fireplace
electric reflections
of flames pretending
to be warmth
where none is possible
except in the comfort
of soft fabric
and the remembered
scent of her perfume.

Longevity

after Kay Ryan

Sorrow makes
a habit of itself.
Meaning
tears persist
no matter
how often
you dry them.
Meaning
memories endure
no matter
how far you try
to push
them away,
no matter
how often
you wish
to hush the heart,
how many times
you pry the art
from the wall,
close the albums
after you tear
out that single photo
to test what
aloneness can bear.

That Tin Box

after Laure-Anne Bosselaar

Black, with Tole-painted flowers,
it had lived on father's dresser
as long as I can remember,
its contents a mystery to us children,
though we were sure it held treasure—
gold coins or silver pins he won at field trials.

After he died, the box came to me,
its top distorted from years of use.
I wrested it open to discover
safety pins, some pencil stubs,
buttons lost from long-ago shirts.
And they remain there still.

We have them, don't we?
Collections of life's relics, tokens,
worthy or worthless—
things we dust from time to time,
peek at now and then
to reassure ourselves.

The Last Photo

Ekphrasis on "Untitled, 1977"
photograph by Mary Elizabeth Ernst

The rooms are sparsely furnished,
lit only by a single, shade-less bulb.
There is seating for several people:
a bench, two wooden chairs
that should invite occupation, but do not.

It is clear the absent people left purposefully.
Before the camera's final shutter,
they took time to clean and polish,
take pictures from the walls,
remove all evidence of lives lived

of all that spoke of comfort or grace.
If any air is moving,
there are no more dreams for it to stir.
A timelessness has settled
that speaks of neither the past nor the future.

In the last photo of my rooms
the remnants of life will linger.
You will see chairs with cushions,
lazy from sitting, half-read books
laying open, art covering the walls.

There will be water rings on the tables,
clutter on the counters,
windows in need of washing.
The air will be unsettled,
old dreams still moving about.

The scene will be weighty with the past
and you will know
I did not leave on purpose.

The Spaces Between Memories

I will never tell you everything
about myself
        only
snippets of the lives I've lived
culled from my heart's ill-kept diary
                rife with erasures
and missing entries
        vacancies where things were forgotten
omitted
    spaces
        where shame and sadness hide.

But you must already know
that even what is here
even what I shared has tears
        and pieces
                worn from the edges.

Notes

Lyrics quoted in "Learning the Lyrics" are from: Ball, Ernest R. and Brennan, J. Keirn, "Let the Rest of the World Go By," 1919.

Poem referenced in "Perhaps a Peach" is from "From Blossoms," Li-Young Lee in *Rose.* Copyright © 1986, Li-Young Lee.

Painting referenced in "Postcard from New York," is *Seated Nude Holding a Flower,* Joan Miró, 1917, on view at The Metropolitan Museum, Fifth Avenue, Gallery 106, New York City, New York.

About the Author

Bonnie Wehle was raised in Upstate New York and in Tucson, Arizona. A graduate of Wellesley College (BA) and the University of Oregon (MS), she worked as an architectural historian for the California Department of Transportation and as an independent historic preservation consultant. She has made her home in several states including New York, Illinois, Oregon, California, Utah, and Arizona.

An ardent student of poetry, Bonnie has had the good fortune to study with several notable poets including Laure-Anne Bosselaar, Ross Gay, Kevin Prufer, Adrian Matejka, Nickole Brown, and Jessica Jacobs. Her work has appeared in *Coal Hill Review, Rockvale Review, River Heron Review, Sky Islands Journal, The Ocotillo Review,* and elsewhere.

She serves as a docent at the University of Arizona Poetry Center, where for many years, she facilitated a monthly poetry circle. Her chapbook, *A Certain Ache: Poems in Women's Voices,* was published in 2022 by Finishing Line Press. She currently lives in Tucson with her dog, Tillie.

Follow more of Bonnie's poetry at:
bonniewehle.com

www.ingramcontent.com/pod-product-compliance
Lightning Source LLC
Chambersburg PA
CBHW031008090426

42737CB00008B/735